THE ELEMENTS

Iron

Giles Sparrow

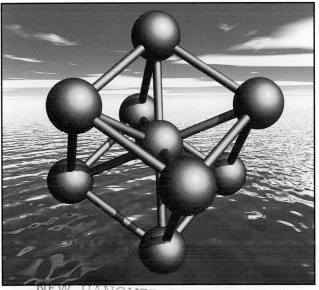

BENCHMARK BOOKS

MARSHALL CAVENDISH

NEW YORK

Benchmark Books
Marshall Cavendish Corporation
99 White Plains Road
Tarrytown, New York 10591-9001

Library of Congress Cataloging-in-Publication Data
Sparrow, Giles.
Iron / by Giles Sparrow.
p.   cm. — (The elements)
Includes index.
Summary: Discusses the origin, discovery, special characteristics,
and uses of iron.
ISBN 0-7614-0880-0 (lib. bdg.)
1. Iron—Juvenile literature. [1. Iron.] I. Title. II. Series: Elements (Benchmark Books)
QD181.F4S63 1999
669'.141—dc21   97-48524 CIP AC

Printed in Hong Kong

Picture credits
Corbis (UK) Ltd: 4, 6, 11, 19, 21, 30.
Science Photo Library: 7, 8, 9, 10, 13, 14, 15, 16, 17, 18, 20, 22, 23, 24, 25, 26, 27.

Series created by Brown Packaging Partworks
Designed by wda

Contents

What is iron?

Iron is one of the most common metals in the world. On its own, it is used to make bridges, automobiles, supports for buildings, machines, and tools. It is mixed with other elements to make alloys, the most important of which is steel. Iron also has an important job inside our bodies, carrying oxygen to where it is needed.

Iron has played a huge part in human history. It was one of the first metals that people learned to extract from rocky ores. Iron was much stronger than any of the other metals known, and iron tools helped to create human civilization.

In the periodic table

Iron has the chemical symbol "Fe." This is taken from its Latin name, ferrum. It is positioned in the middle section of the periodic table, surrounded by other metals including nickel, copper, silver, and gold. Iron and its neighbors in the table are called transition metals, and they all have similar properties.

Inside the atom

Everything you can see around you is made up of particles called atoms, which are almost unimaginably tiny. If 10 million atoms were lined up, side by side, they would only measure $\frac{1}{25}$ in (1 mm)!

Inside each atom are even smaller particles: protons, neutrons, and electrons. The protons and neutrons cluster together in the nucleus at the center of the atom. The electrons spin round the nucleus in a series of layers called electron shells.

The number of protons is given by the atomic number. Iron has an atomic number of 26, which means each atom has 26 protons. The protons and neutrons combine to give the atom its mass. Iron has an atomic mass of 56, which tells us there are 30 neutrons.

Iron compounds are used to build bridges, including Golden Gate Bridge in San Francisco, California.

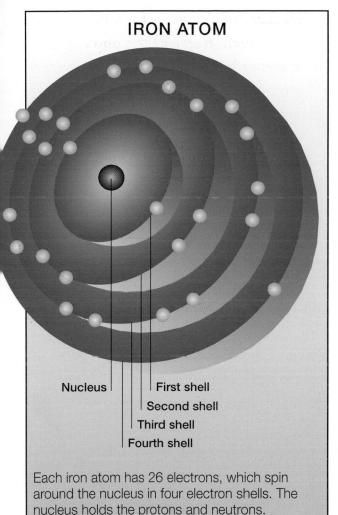

IRON ATOM

Nucleus | First shell
Second shell
Third shell
Fourth shell

Each iron atom has 26 electrons, which spin around the nucleus in four electron shells. The nucleus holds the protons and neutrons.

elements, the outermost shell is not complete. Only a full shell is stable, so elements share or exchange electrons to try and gain a complete outer shell.

The innermost shell can hold up to two electrons. The second can hold up to eight, while the third shell can take up to eighteen and the fourth, up to thirty two.

In the transition metals, the electron shells fill up in an unusual way. The outermost shell always contains two electrons. The remaining electrons go into the preceding shell.

Protons have a positive electrical charge, electrons have a negative charge, while neutrons have no charge. The numbers of electrons and protons are always equal, so there are 26 electrons.

The electrons fill up electron shells from the center. As one shell fills, the electrons go into the next shell out. In most

This modern building (Javitts Center in New York City) is made entirely of steel and glass.

Special characteristics

Pure iron is a silvery metal with a shiny surface. It is a good conductor of heat and electricity, meaning that heat and electricity flow easily through it. Many metals share these characteristics, which are caused by the way millions of individual atoms join together.

The metal atoms are packed in a regular pattern called a metal crystal. The atoms in the crystal are held together by a special kind of attraction called a metal bond. Each atom gives up its outer electrons, which float around the crystal. Because the positively charged protons inside each atom are no longer balanced by negatively charged electrons, the iron atoms have a positive charge. The whole structure is held together by attractions between the positive charges on the atoms and the negative electron "sea."

A piece of iron seen under a powerful microscope. The microscope has magnified the iron 60 times.

Freedom to roam

It is the electrons' freedom to move around that gives metals their properties. Metals are good conductors of electricity because the electrons can flow through the whole metal structure, carrying the electricity with them. Heat is quickly conducted from one edge of the metal to the other. Heating the metal gives the electrons more energy, which makes them move more quickly, carrying the heat with them through the whole material.

The shiny surface is caused by the way light bounces off the loose electrons in the crystal structure. The light hits the metal surface and bounces off in many different directions, just as sunlight is reflected by the waves on the ocean.

Strong bonds

The crystal bonding in the metal is very strong. The atoms are held tightly in place, and iron has to be heated to an incredible

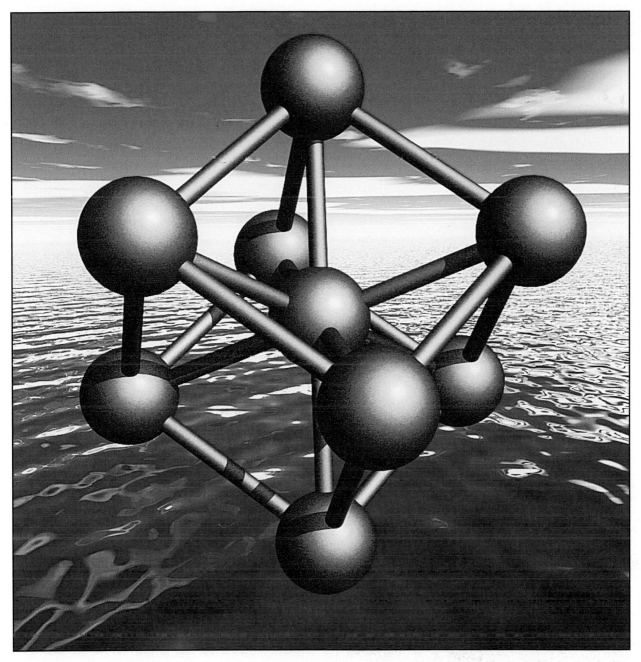

This computer artwork shows how iron atoms are packed together in a regular pattern inside the metal.

2,795°F (1,535°C) before the atoms are pulled out of their places in the metal structure. At this temperature, iron turns to liquid (melts). Liquid iron must be heated even further to 4,982°F (2,750°C) before it will boil (turn to vapor). But pure iron is also quite soft, as the layers of atoms can slip past each other. As a result, iron is said to be ductile, which means it can be easily pulled out into wires.

An exploding star, or supernova. Most of the iron in the universe was created in stars such as this.

Where iron is found

Iron is one of the most commonplace elements on Earth. It is the second most abundant metal, after aluminum, and the fourth most abundant element in Earth's crust. Iron is too reactive to exist on its own. It is always found in the crust mixed together with other elements in compounds called ores.

The main ores that contain iron are hematite, magnetite, and siderite. These are found all round the world, but large deposits exist in Australia, Canada, France, India, South Africa, and the United States. These ores are the main source of the metal in industry.

Iron is also found in a compound called marcasite, which is used to make jewelry. But iron is so common that most minerals in Earth's crust contain at least a trace.

Our planet's hot interior, the core, is about 90 percent iron. Although most of the iron at the surface is locked away in ores, the temperatures deep inside Earth are high enough for the iron to melt.

Earth turns slowly around its axis like an enormous spinning top. As the molten iron shifts about inside Earth's core, it turns the planet into a giant magnet. Invisible lines of magnetic force spread out around the planet, joining at two points that we cannot see on a map: the north magnetic pole and the south magnetic pole.

Iron in space

Iron is quite common in space, even though none of it was formed during the "Big Bang" that created the universe.

All the iron that exists today has been created over billions of years by exploding stars called supernovae. These are the largest stars known—around 50 times more massive than our own Sun. Like all stars, they make energy in nuclear reactions that "fuse" light elements such as hydrogen and helium together to make heavier ones.

Most stars can only produce fairly light elements, but the biggest stars can make heavier and heavier elements, right up to iron. However, when these stars try to use the iron as a fuel, the iron is too heavy and the stars explode.

METEORITE FACTS

● The largest known meteorite lies at Hoba West in Namibia, Africa. It is thought to weigh over 66 tons (60 tonnes)!

● Although fragments of iron have been found at the 0.8-mile (1.3-km) Meteor Crater, Arizona, attempts to mine it have failed.

● A 19th-century czar of Russia had a sword made for him using iron from a meteorite.

Most of the iron in Earth's crust is found in ores. This is hematite, a mixture of iron and oxygen.

The elements created in these explosions are scattered across space and can form nebulae, clouds of gas and dust out of which new stars and planets form.

Meteors and meteorites

When our solar system formed, much of the debris left behind was rich in iron. This material is now scattered through space as asteroids and meteoroids. Sometimes, these space objects fall toward Earth. Some burn up in the atmosphere—we see them as shooting stars or meteors. Some chunks survive the journey through the atmosphere and reach the ground, where they are called "meteorites."

The most common meteorites contain about 90 percent iron. Iron from meteorites has larger crystals than iron formed on Earth. Experts have identified ancient tools and jewelry made from meteorite fragments, signs of humanity's first encounters with iron.

A meteor falling to Earth. The meteor burns as it hurtles through the atmosphere and appears as a bright streak in the sky.

How iron was discovered

In ancient times, people knew iron only as a metal that fell from the sky. The first metals that people learned to work, making tools and ornaments, were gold, copper, and tin, which could be found as pure nuggets in areas around the eastern Mediterranean Sea. These metals were very soft, and tools and instruments made from them would not have lasted very long.

Making iron tools

The earliest iron tools were made around 3,000 to 2,000 B.C.E., most likely by hammering and heating iron from meteorites. The discovery of "smelting" (the way to extract iron from its ores) was probably accidental. Perhaps some ancient metalworkers lit a fire on top of rocks that contained iron ore and recognized the resulting metal as iron.

Extracting iron

Iron was extracted by burning the ore with charcoal (a very carbon-rich fuel). The carbon in the charcoal forms carbon dioxide gas by reacting with the oxygen from the iron ore, leaving behind soft, spongy iron and a mixture of impurities.

DID YOU KNOW?

THE ASHOKA PILLAR

Near Delhi, India, stands a tall iron pillar. It was built around 1,500 years ago as a memorial to the Emperor Ashoka. The pillar seems to be made of remarkably pure iron, but it has never rusted (see page 18). Experts are still arguing today about what keeps it in this condition.

Sometimes, the impurities in the iron ores would have produced metal that was stronger and more hard-wearing than the normal iron. These discoveries eventually led to the first steels.

The secret of making iron gradually spread out from the Mediterranean, until, around 500 B.C.E., it was known across all of Europe, the Middle East, and North Africa. Iron ore was much more widespread than copper and tin, and iron tools were so common at this time that historians call the period the Iron Age.

The spear at the top left of the page and the sickle and the axe head shown here are all made of iron. Early people learned how to work iron around 3,000 years ago, leading to the period of history called the Iron Age.

Magnetism

Mention the word "magnetism" and you probably think of the way a compass needle swings to point north or how a horseshoe magnet can pick up metal objects. Both these forms of magnetism and others are caused by the special properties of iron—the way it can create or be affected by an invisible magnetic field.

Shifting charge

Magnetism in iron is created because the electrons inside the atoms are not evenly distributed in their shells. As the balance of the charge shifts from side to side, this creates tiny atomic magnets called magnetic dipoles.

The atoms of many different elements form dipoles, but only iron, cobalt, and nickel are strongly magnetic, and iron is the most magnetic of the three. This is because the crystalline structure of the

The magnetic field around two bar magnets becomes clear when iron filings are scattered near the magnets.

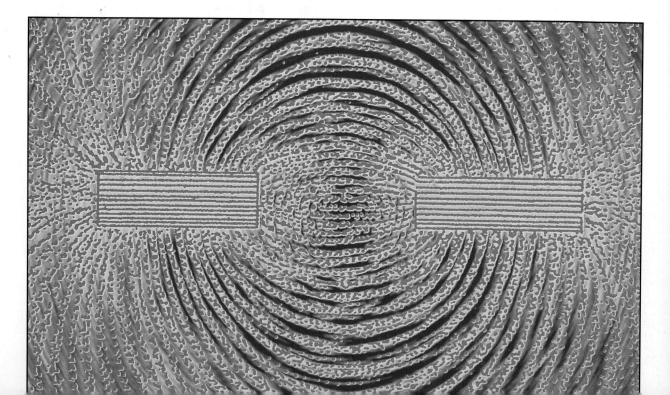

Some magnets are so strong they can be used to lift automobile parts in scrap yards.

ATOMS AT WORK

In a piece of iron, the atoms line up within small regions called domains. But the different domains are pointing in lots of different directions.

Unmagnetized

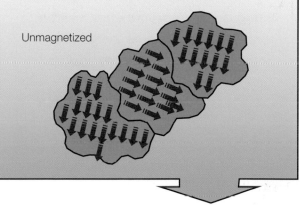

When iron is magnetized, the domains are pulled by the magnetic field so that they all point in the same direction.

Magnetized

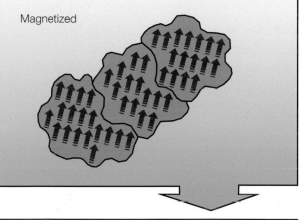

The magnetism lasts until the iron is heated or hit hard. Two other metals also have magnetic domains. These are nickel and cobalt, which are iron's neighbors in the periodic table. However, the magnetic effect remains strongest in iron.

atoms in iron is very special. The atoms are spaced just the right distance apart for the dipoles to affect one another strongly. The dipoles line up and form small magnetic areas called domains.

The magnetic domains within a piece of iron usually point in different directions and cancel each other out. But if the iron is placed in a magnetic field, the domains are pulled in the same direction and the metal becomes a magnet.

The magnetism does not last forever. When the iron is removed from the magnetic field, the domains flip back toward their normal positions.

MAKE YOUR OWN COMPASS

It is easy to make your own compass using an ordinary sewing needle, a magnet, and some polystyrene packing. This is what you do:

● Magnetize your needle by running a magnet along it. You'll have to do this a number of times and always move the magnet in the same direction. Check to see if your needle has been magnetized by using it to pick up another needle.

● Cut a circle out of a thin piece of polystyrene packing. Stick the magnetized needle onto the middle of the polystyrene with glue or tape.

● Fill a bowl with water, and gently place the polystyrene onto the surface of the water so that it floats. Turn the bowl around. Whichever way you move it, the needle should swing to line up with Earth's north-south magnetic field.

● The earliest compasses, invented by the Chinese in the 12th century, worked just like yours. The Chinese called them magic fish!

This monorail train floats above the track. It is held in position by powerful magnets.

The magnetism can also be destroyed by heating the metal to above 1,410°F (766°C) or by hitting it hard. But the iron never quite returns to its original state. If it is exposed to a strong magnetic field repeatedly, any normal piece of iron can be turned into a magnet.

DID YOU KNOW?

LODESTONES

The iron ore magnetite is naturally magnetic. In the Middle Ages, navigators used it to make compasses. When a lump of magnetite was hung from a thread, it would move to point north. The ore was given the name "lodestone" from an old word "lode," which means "way." Large magnetite deposits can be magnetic enough to confuse compasses, drawing ships and airplanes off their course.

How iron reacts

The way an element reacts depends on the number of electrons in its outer electron shell. All elements want their outer electron shell to be full, because this makes the atom more stable. Chemical reactions are really a way of losing or gaining electrons to get a complete outer shell.

Iron reacts by donating either two or three electrons to atoms of other elements. The transfer of the electrons forms chemical bonds, which hold the atoms together in compounds.

The compounds that form when iron loses two electrons are called ferric. When iron loses three electrons, the compounds are called ferrous. Some compounds are a mixture—they contain some iron atoms that have lost two electrons and others that have lost three.

A piece of magnetite. Magnetite contains iron atoms that have lost two and three electrons.

ATOMS AT WORK

Hydrogen chloride contains an atom of hydrogen joined to an atom of chlorine. Iron sulfide has iron attached to sulfur.

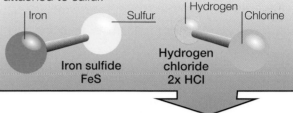

Iron sulfide
FeS

Hydrogen chloride
2x HCl

When hydrogen chloride dissolves in water, the bond between the atoms breaks and the atoms float apart. Hydrogen chloride in water is hydrochloric acid. The more hydrogen chloride the water contains, the stronger the acid.

When iron sulfide is added to the acid, the atoms are exchanged. The iron joins with the chlorine to give iron chloride. The hydrogen attaches to the sulfur to make hydrogen sulfide. This is a poisonous gas with the smell of rotten eggs.

Iron chloride
$FeCl_2$

Hydrogen sulfide
H_2S

The reaction between iron sulfide and hydrochloric acid looks like this:

$FeS + 2HCl \rightarrow H_2S + FeCl_2$

This tells us that one molecule of iron sulfide reacts with two molecules of hydrogen chloride to give one molecule of hydrogen sulfide and one molecule of iron chloride.

Atoms that lose or gain electrons are called ions. Because the number of electrons and protons no longer balance, ions have an electrical charge. If an atom loses electrons, there are more protons than electrons, so the ion has a positive charge. An atom that gains electrons has more electrons than protons, so its electrical charge is negative.

Reactions with oxygen

Iron forms three compounds with oxygen. Ferrous oxide (chemical formula FeO) is a black powder that explodes in air. The second oxide has caused problems for as long as people have made things out of

DID YOU KNOW?

WRITING ABOUT IRON COMPOUNDS
A Roman number in parentheses is often included in the names of iron compounds to show how many electrons the iron has lost to another atom. Ferrous oxide contains iron that has donated two electrons. It can be written iron (II) oxide. Ferric oxide is written iron (III) oxide to show that each atom of iron has lost three electrons. Magnetite contains both types of iron, so it is written as iron (II, III) oxide.

iron. Its chemical name is ferric oxide (Fe_2O_3), but we know it better as rust. The third oxide is the black iron ore, magnetite, which contains both types of ions. Magnetite has the formula Fe_3O_4.

Reactions with other nonmetals

Most of the other nonmetals react with iron. Compounds that contain a metal joined to a nonmetal are called salts. Iron reacts with chlorine to give the salt iron chloride ($FeCl_2$), with fluorine to give iron fluoride ($FeFl_2$), and with sulfur to give iron sulfide (FeS).

Iron and its compounds will also react with acids, such as hydrochloric acid, to create new combinations.

The flask on the left contains iron sulfate. After ammonium hexacyanoferrate is added, the solution turns from yellow to bright red. This is a test for iron (III) ions.

Bright colors

Many iron compounds dissolve in water creating brightly colored solutions. The iron ions become surrounded by a cage of water molecules. Iron (II) ions give a bluish green solution, while iron (III) ions are yellow. Color differences are a good way of telling the two ions apart.

One of the chemical tests involves potassium thiocyanate, a compound that contains potassium, sulfur, carbon, and nitrogen atoms. If potassium thiocyanate is added to a solution containing iron (III) ions, the solution turns deep red. But if potassium thiocyanate is added to iron (II) ions, the color stays the same. This test is very sensitive. It works even if the amount of iron (III) is tiny.

Displacement reactions

Iron is very reactive, and it will force less reactive metals out of their compounds. This type of reaction is called a displacement reaction because the iron displaces another element and takes its place in the compound.

A displacement reaction occurs when iron filings are dissolved into a beaker of blue copper sulfate solution. The iron pushes the copper out of the way and joins with the sulfate to give iron sulfate. This compound is pale green, so the color of the solution changes. The copper metal falls to the bottom of the glass.

ATOMS AT WORK

Copper sulfate is a compound that has one atom of copper joined to a sulfate ion, which is made of one sulfur atom and four oxygen atoms. Copper sulfate dissolves in water to give a bright blue solution.

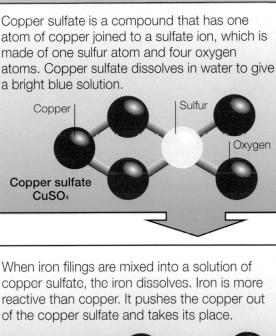

Copper sulfate
$CuSO_4$

When iron filings are mixed into a solution of copper sulfate, the iron dissolves. Iron is more reactive than copper. It pushes the copper out of the copper sulfate and takes its place.

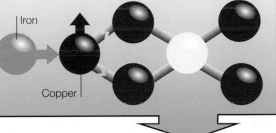

Pale-green iron sulfate solution forms. The copper falls to the bottom of the glass.

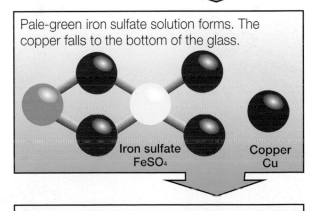

Iron sulfate
$FeSO_4$ Copper
                  Cu

This is an example of a displacement reaction. It can be written like this:

Fe + CuSO₄ → FeSO₄ + Cu

$$Fe + CuSO_4 \rightarrow FeSO_4 + Cu$$

The iron and the copper have swapped places.

Rust

One thing everyone knows about iron is that if you leave it out in the rain for long enough, it goes rusty. But rust forms in a chemical reaction, and knowing about the way iron reacts helps find ways of slowing or stopping rusting.

Rusting occurs when iron is attacked by water that has molecules of oxygen gas dissolved in it. A chemical reaction takes place between the iron and the oxygen. This results in ferric oxide, a brown, crumbly compound. Ferric oxide has two iron atoms attached to three atoms of oxygen, and its chemical formula is written like this: Fe_2O_3.

A pile of rusting automobiles. Rust forms when iron reacts with oxygen from the air or water.

Rust develops most quickly on rough or cracked iron objects. These objects have a larger area for the chemical reaction to occur and places where water can collect. The rate of rusting also depends on how much oxygen the water contains.

How to stop rust

The easiest way to prevent rusting is to cover the iron surface with a coating that stops the water and oxygen from reaching the metal. Coatings range from paints to elaborate enamels. They work fine unless the surface cracks, which lets water and oxygen seep through.

SEE FOR YOURSELF

WHICH RUSTS FIRST?

You can find out what causes rusting with this simple experiment.

● Find three jars. Fill two of them with tap water and leave the third jar empty. Pour a teaspoon of salt into one of the water jars and stir until all the salt has dissolved.

● Now put a piece of steel wool into each jar and leave them.

● Leave the jars for a few days and check them regularly. You should find that the iron in the salt water rusts first. The salt speeds up the rusting in just the same way that iron rusts faster when it is exposed to seaspray on the coast.

Galvanized steel scrap waiting to be recycled. Rust has formed where the zinc has worn away.

A much better way to prevent rusting is by coating the iron with another metal that is more attractive to the oxygen atoms than the iron is. The oxygen atoms attack the other metal and leave the iron alone. The second metal is sometimes called a sacrificial metal because it is "sacrificed" to save the iron.

The most common choice is zinc. A method called galvanizing coats iron objects, such as trashcans, with a layer of zinc. When exposed to the weather, the rainwater attacks the zinc rather than the iron, turning it into zinc oxide. The iron will be protected for as long as any zinc remains on the surface.

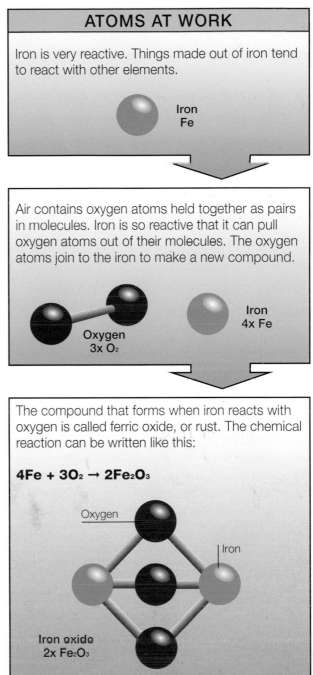

ATOMS AT WORK

Iron is very reactive. Things made out of iron tend to react with other elements.

Iron
Fe

Air contains oxygen atoms held together as pairs in molecules. Iron is so reactive that it can pull oxygen atoms out of their molecules. The oxygen atoms join to the iron to make a new compound.

Oxygen
3x O_2

Iron
4x Fe

The compound that forms when iron reacts with oxygen is called ferric oxide, or rust. The chemical reaction can be written like this:

$$4Fe + 3O_2 \rightarrow 2Fe_2O_3$$

Oxygen

Iron

Iron oxide
2x Fe_2O_3

But the best way of stopping iron from rusting is to mix its atoms with those of another metal to make steel. Today, various types of steel have largely replaced pure iron in manufacturing.

Iron in the body

Most living creatures need small traces of metals in their diet to keep them healthy, but iron is probably the most important of all—we could not live without it. This is because iron is a vital part of the chemicals that make up blood and allow it to transport life-giving oxygen around our bodies.

Most of the iron in our diet is used to make one particular compound, a protein

NUTRITION FACTS

● Doctors recommend a daily intake of 14 mg of iron.

● Good sources of iron include red meat, fish, egg yolks, green vegetables, legumes such as beans and peas, and whole grains.

● About 70 percent of the iron in the human body is found in red blood cells.

● Iron is also an important nutrient for plants, where it helps with photosynthesis (the process in which plants use sunlight to make food).

Red blood cells carry oxygen round the body. They can do this because they contain iron.

called hemoglobin, which is found in red blood cells. Each hemoglobin molecule contains four iron atoms. As blood passes through the lungs, oxygen attaches itself to the iron in the hemoglobin, changing the blood's color from dark to bright red. The oxygen travels through the body to where it is needed.

A useful molecule

Hemoglobin is a very useful molecule. As it moves from oxygen-rich to oxygen-poor areas of the body, it changes shape, allowing it to absorb or release more oxygen. Changes to the hemoglobin alter the way it works in different animals. Half the molecule in fish hemoglobin matches the human version, while chimp hemoglobin is identical to the human type.

We all need a small amount of iron in our diet. Lettuces are a good source of iron. Other iron-rich foods include red meat, fish, and eggs.

Lacking iron

People who don't get enough iron from their diet can fall ill. If the iron level in our bodies falls too low, we can suffer from anemia. This causes tiredness, muscle weakness, and loss of concentration.

Pregnant women are particularly likely to get anemia, as the developing baby raids the mother's stores of iron to make its own hemoglobin.

Mild anemia can be cured by eating more iron rich foods. In more serious cases, it is treated by taking iron tablets.

DID YOU KNOW?

IRON EATERS
You may have heard the expression "cast-iron stomach." There are some tiny creatures for whom this is literally true! Certain bacteria eat iron and use it for energy. Despite their size, microorganisms reproduce with amazing speed. If they find a rich source of food, these iron bacteria grow into large masses that can block water pipes.

Making iron

The basic method for extracting iron has stayed more or less the same for thousands of years. The main sources are the oxides magnetite (Fe_3O_4) and hematite (Fe_2O_3), and siderite (iron carbonate, $FeCO_3$). Most iron ores are near Earth's surface, so they are easily removed by quarrying.

The ores are melted down in a blast furnace, a tall stack about 100 ft (30 m) high and 26 ft (8 m) across the bottom. The temperature at the bottom of the furnace is a fiery 3,450°F (1,900°C).

Iron ore is poured into the top of the furnace along with coke, a very carbon-rich fuel. Limestone (calcium carbonate) is added to help remove impurities.

Blasts of air are pumped in through holes in the bottom of the furnace. The air melts the coke and ore mixture as it falls through the furnace. The burning coke pulls the oxygen out of the iron ore, leaving molten iron behind.

The limestone reacts with impurities in the iron to form a scummy mixture called slag. A layer of molten slag floats on top of the molten iron and is removed from the furnace from time to time.

The temperature inside a blast furnace is so high that the molten metal glows.

The molten iron is tapped from the furnace and poured into molds of sand. When it cools and becomes solid, the iron forms a central bar with little bars sticking out the side. This looks a bit like a female pig nursing a litter of piglets, so the iron became known as pig iron.

Different types

Despite the limestone, pig iron still contains impurities. This makes it brittle and hard to work. It can be made purer by heating it with hematite and limestone to drive off more of the impurities. This creates iron that is 99.5 percent pure. Called wrought iron, it is used to make chains and gates. Wrought iron is tougher than pig iron but easier to shape.

Most of the iron produced in blast furnaces is just the starting point for an even more useful material—steel.

These girders contain iron. They are used to make the frameworks of buildings and bridges.

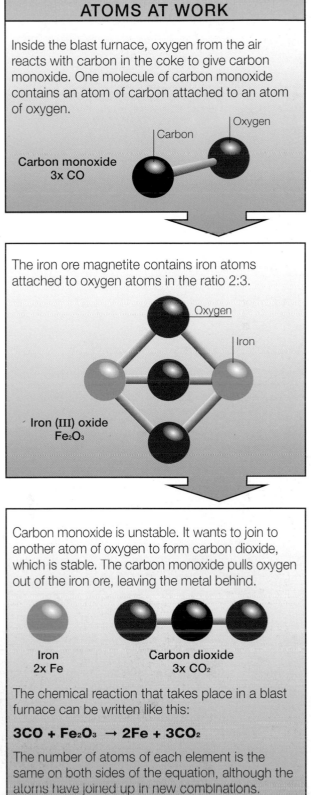

ATOMS AT WORK

Inside the blast furnace, oxygen from the air reacts with carbon in the coke to give carbon monoxide. One molecule of carbon monoxide contains an atom of carbon attached to an atom of oxygen.

Oxygen

Carbon

Carbon monoxide
3x CO

The iron ore magnetite contains iron atoms attached to oxygen atoms in the ratio 2:3.

Oxygen

Iron

Iron (III) oxide
Fe_2O_3

Carbon monoxide is unstable. It wants to join to another atom of oxygen to form carbon dioxide, which is stable. The carbon monoxide pulls oxygen out of the iron ore, leaving the metal behind.

Iron
2x Fe

Carbon dioxide
3x CO_2

The chemical reaction that takes place in a blast furnace can be written like this:

$3CO + Fe_2O_3 \rightarrow 2Fe + 3CO_2$

The number of atoms of each element is the same on both sides of the equation, although the atoms have joined up in new combinations.

Uses of iron

Everyone knows that iron is used in building and engineering, but it also turns up in lots of everyday places.

Iron plays an important role in the body, so it is not surprising that iron is found in medicines. Tincture of iron is iron chloride (FeCl) dissolved in alcohol. It is used to treat anemia and as an astringent—a chemical that pulls bodily tissues together, allowing them to heal.

Magnetic tapes

Ferric oxide (Fe_2O_3) is magnetic and chemically very stable. Powdered ferric oxide is used to make the coating on magnetic recording tape.

An engineer working in a recording studio. Sound is recorded onto tape that has a coating of ferric oxide.

Tapes record sound by registering changes in the sound frequencies. These shifts in the frequency change the direction of magnetic particles on the tape, making a record of the sound.

Different colors

Many iron compounds are brightly colored. They are used to make dyes to color textiles. Iron-based dyes join to the material with a chemical bond, so they are fixed tight. This creates a color that lasts for a long time and does not fade when the fabric is washed.

A particularly useful compound is ferrous sulfate, also known as green vitriol. This was used in ancient Greece and Rome to make ink. It still has this use today, but it is also an ingredient of fertilizers and pesticides.

Ferric oxide is the starting point for pigments (colored compounds) that range from yellow to deep red. The red form is called Venetian red.

Building with iron

At one time, iron was the main structural material in the world. It is still used to make things such as engine blocks, domestic stoves, chains, and gates.

Iron is very strong, but it is also brittle and likely to rust. Today, iron has been largely replaced in the construction industry by steel.

Steel

Steel is an alloy—a mixture in which atoms of another element are spread evenly through the crystal structure of the iron. These other atoms make the steel quite different from iron.

Early methods

The methods for making steel were kept secret for hundreds of years, because steel was used to manufacture sword blades. The first large-scale method was invented around 1850 by English industrialist Henry Bessemer (1813–1898). His furnace was a large iron barrel, lined with heat-resistant bricks. The whole structure was mounted on a pivot.

Bessemer's process involved melting ingots of pig iron with limestone then blowing air through the mixture at high speeds. Oxygen in the air reacted with

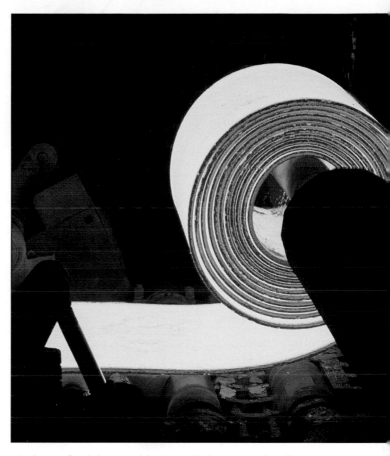

A sheet of red-hot steel being rolled in a steel mill. The sheets are later cut into different shapes for use.

impurities in the iron and blew them out of the furnace as waste. Other elements required for making steel could be added to the purified metal, before the mix was tapped off and cast.

Modern processes

The main problem with the Bessemer process was that bubbles of nitrogen became trapped inside the steel. This made the steel weak and brittle. Today's steelmakers still use the same basic method, but the air has been replaced by pure oxygen, blown through the molten metal at supersonic speeds. Finished steel ingots are processed in a mill, where they are heated and passed through heavy rollers to create sheets that can be cut into different shapes and sizes.

Different steels

There are several different types of steel, depending on which other chemical element is added to the iron. The other element gives the steel certain physical properties, which in turn determines how the material is used.

The most common steels are the carbon steels, which contain anything from 0.05 to 1.5 percent carbon. Carbon atoms are larger than iron ones. When they are trapped in the crystalline structure of the metal, they act as

blocks, stopping layers of iron from sliding past each other. This makes the steel strong. The downside of this is that the steel is harder to work and can shatter if it is subjected to a large enough shock.

Carbon steels are the ones most commonly used to make automobile bodies, ships, knives, machinery, and structural supports inside buildings.

Alloy steels contain elements other than carbon. They are more expensive to produce than carbon steel but have more varied uses.

Low alloy steels contain from 1 to 5 percent of another metal. Nickel is used if the steel has to stand up to being pulled. Nickel steels are the basis of products ranging from long-span bridges to bicycle chains. Tungsten is the best metal if the steel is going to operate at

The Eiffel Tower in Paris, France, was built in 1889 out of iron. Today, a construction such as this is more likely to be made of steel.

high temperatures. High speed drills are made from this type of steel.

High alloy steels contain from 12 to 18 percent of the other metal. They are more expensive to manufacture than low alloy steels, so they are only used for very special purposes where strength and reliability are important—such as making aircraft parts.

Stainless steels are a familiar group of high alloy steels. These contain chromium and nickel, which make the steel strong and resistant to corrosion.

DID YOU KNOW?

HENRY BESSEMER

Englishman Henry Bessemer (1813–1898) patented more than 100 inventions in his lifetime. When nobody would back his steel production method, he went into business himself. Bessemer undercut his rivals (sold his products more cheaply than theirs) until they bought licenses for his process. This made him very rich, and he retired from the steel industry at the age of 56. There are six towns and cities in the United States named after him!

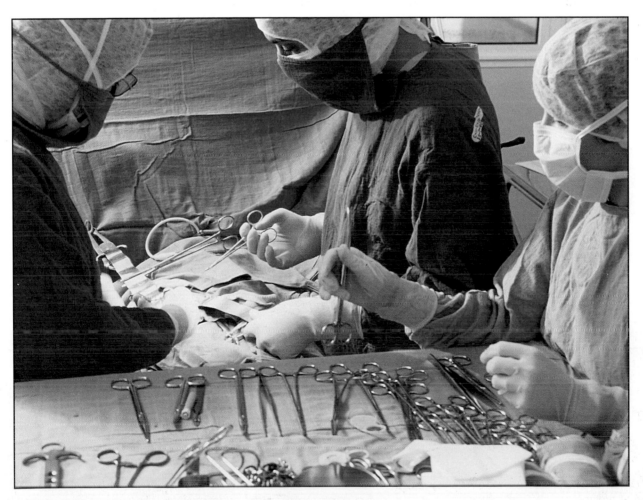

Stainless steels do not rust. They are used to make surgical instruments and cooking utensils.

Periodic table

Everything in the universe is made from combinations of substances called elements. Elements are the building blocks of matter. They are made of tiny atoms, which are much too small to see.

The character of an atom depends on how many even tinier particles called protons there are in its center, or nucleus. An element's atomic number is the same as the number of protons.

Scientists have found around 110 different elements. About 90 elements occur naturally on Earth. The rest have been made in experiments.

All these elements are set out on a chart called the periodic table. This lists all the elements in order according to their atomic number.

The elements at the left of the table are metals. Those at the right are nonmetals. Between the metals and the nonmetals are the metalloids, which sometimes act like metals and sometimes like nonmetals.

- On the left of the table are the alkali metals. These elements have just one electron in their outer shells.

- On the right of the periodic table are the noble gases. These elements have full outer shells.

- Elements in the same group have the same number of electrons in their outer shells.

- Elements get more reactive as you go down a group.

- The number of electrons orbiting the nucleus increases down each group.

- The transition metals are in the middle of the table, between Groups II and III.

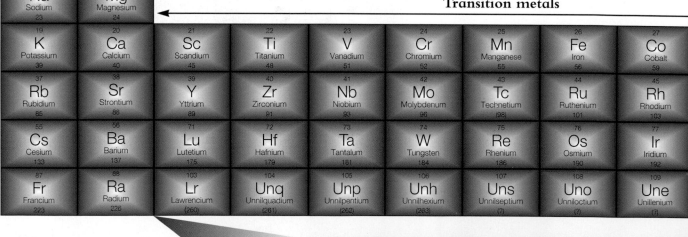

Group I

Group II

Transition metals

1 H Hydrogen 1								
3 Li Lithium 7	4 Be Beryllium 9							
11 Na Sodium 23	12 Mg Magnesium 24							
19 K Potassium 39	20 Ca Calcium 40	21 Sc Scandium 45	22 Ti Titanium 48	23 V Vanadium 51	24 Cr Chromium 52	25 Mn Manganese 55	26 Fe Iron 56	27 Co Cobalt 59
37 Rb Rubidium 85	38 Sr Strontium 88	39 Y Yttrium 89	40 Zr Zirconium 91	41 Nb Niobium 93	42 Mo Molybdenum 96	43 Tc Technetium (98)	44 Ru Ruthenium 101	45 Rh Rhodium 103
55 Cs Cesium 133	56 Ba Barium 137	71 Lu Lutetium 175	72 Hf Hafnium 179	73 Ta Tantalum 181	74 W Tungsten 184	75 Re Rhenium 186	76 Os Osmium 190	77 Ir Iridium 192
87 Fr Francium 223	88 Ra Radium 226	103 Lr Lawrencium (260)	104 Unq Unnilquadium (261)	105 Unp Unnilpentium (262)	106 Unh Unnilhexium (263)	107 Uns Unnilseptium (?)	108 Uno Unniloctium (?)	109 Une Unilenium (?)

Lanthanide elements

Actinide elements

| 57 La Lanthanum 39 | 58 Ce Cerium 140 | 59 Pr Praseodymium 141 | 60 Nd Neodymium 144 | 61 Pm Promethium (145) |
| 89 Ac Actinium 227 | 90 Th Thorium 232 | 91 Pa Protactinium 231 | 92 U Uranium 238 | 93 Np Neptunium (237) |

The horizontal rows are called periods. As you go across a period, the atomic number increases by one from each element to the next. The vertical columns are called groups. Elements get heavier as you go down a group. All the elements in a group have the same number of electrons in their outer shells. This means they react in similar ways.

The transition metals fall between Groups II and III. Their electron shells fill up in an unusual way. The lanthanide elements and the actinide elements are set apart from the main table to make it easier to read. All the lanthanide elements and the actinide elements are quite rare.

Iron in the table

Iron has atomic number 26, so it has 26 protons in its nucleus. It is positioned in the middle of the table among the group of metals termed the transition metals.

Like many other metals, iron is shiny and a good conductor of electricity and heat. It is very reactive and forms compounds with most of the nonmetals.

- ▨ Metals
- ▨ Metalloids (semimetals)
- ▨ Nonmetals

26	
Fe	Atomic (proton) number
Iron	Symbol
56	Name
	Atomic mass

Group VIII

			Group III	Group IV	Group V	Group VI	Group VII	2 He Helium 4
			5 B Boron 11	6 C Carbon 12	7 N Nitrogen 14	8 O Oxygen 16	9 F Fluorine 19	10 Ne Neon 20
			13 Al Aluminum 27	14 Si Silicon 28	15 P Phosphorus 31	16 S Sulfur 32	17 Cl Chlorine 35	18 Ar Argon 40
28 Ni Nickel 59	29 Cu Copper 64	30 Zn Zinc 65	31 Ga Gallium 70	32 Ge Germanium 73	33 As Arsenic 75	34 Se Selenium 79	35 Br Bromine 80	36 Kr Krypton 84
46 Pd Palladium 106	47 Ag Silver 108	48 Cd Cadmium 112	49 In Indium 115	50 Sn Tin 119	51 Sb Antimony 122	52 Te Tellurium 128	53 I Iodine 127	54 Xe Xenon 131
78 Pt Platinum 195	79 Au Gold 197	80 Hg Mercury 201	81 Tl Thallium 204	82 Pb Lead 207	83 Bi Bismuth 209	84 Po Polonium (209)	85 At Astatine (210)	86 Rn Radon (222)

62 Sm Samarium 150	63 Eu Europium 152	64 Gd Gadolinium 157	65 Tb Terbium 159	66 Dy Dysprosium 163	67 Ho Holmium 165	68 Er Erbium 167	69 Tm Thulium 169	70 Yb Ytterbium 173
94 Pu Plutonium (244)	95 Am Americium (243)	96 Cm Curium (247)	97 Bk Berkelium (247)	98 Cf Californium (251)	99 Es Einsteinium (252)	100 Fm Fermium (257)	101 Md Mendelevium (258)	102 No Nobelium (259)

Chemical reactions

Chemical reactions are going on around us all the time. Some reactions involve just two substances; others many more. But whenever a reaction takes place, at least one substance is changed.

In a chemical reaction, the atoms stay the same. But they join up in different combinations to form new molecules.

Writing an equation

Chemical reactions can be described by writing down the atoms and molecules

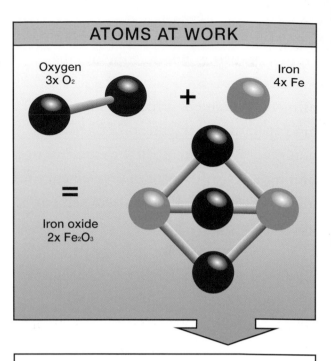

ATOMS AT WORK

Oxygen
$3x O_2$

Iron
$4x Fe$

$=$

Iron oxide
$2x Fe_2O_3$

The chemical reaction that takes place when iron rusts is written like this:

$4Fe + 3O_2 \rightarrow 2Fe_2O_3$

The number of iron and oxygen atoms is the same on both sides of the equation.

Rust forms when iron metal reacts with oxygen. The reaction occurs faster in saltwater.

before and the atoms and molecules after. Since the atoms stay the same, the number of atoms before will be the same as the number of atoms after. Chemists write the reaction as an equation.

Making it balance

When the number of each atoms on both sides of the equation is equal, the equation is balanced. If the number is not equal, something must be wrong. So the chemist adjusts the number of atoms involved until the equation balances.

Glossary

alloy: A mixture of a metal with one or more other elements. Steel is an example of an iron alloy.

atom: The smallest part of an element that still has all the properties of that element.

atomic number: The number of protons in an atom.

bond: The attraction between two atoms that holds the atoms together.

compound: A substance that is made of atoms of more than one element. The atoms in a molecule are held together by chemical bonds.

electron: A tiny particle with a negative charge. Electrons are found inside atoms, where they move around the nucleus in layers called electron shells.

hemoglobin: A protein that is found inside red blood cells. Hemoglobin contains atoms of iron. It is used to carry oxygen around the body.

ion: An atom that has lost or gained electrons. Ions have either a positive or a negative electrical charge.

metal: An element on the left of the periodic table. Metals are good conductors of heat and electricity.

molecule: A particle that contains atoms held together by chemical bonds.

neutron: A tiny particle with no electrical charge found in the nucleus of an atom.

nonmetal: An element at the right hand side of the periodic table. Nonmetals are liquids or gases at normal temperatures. They are poor at conducting heat and electricity.

nucleus: The center of an atom. It contains protons and neutrons.

ore: A compound that contains a useful element, usually a metal, mixed together with other elements.

periodic table: A chart of all the chemical elements laid out in order of their atomic number.

products: The substances formed in a chemical reaction.

proton: A tiny particle with a positive charge. Protons are found inside the nucleus of an atom.

reactants: The substances that react together in a chemical reaction.

rust: The crumbly brown substance that forms on the surface of iron. Rust is actually ferric oxide and it forms as the result of a chemical reaction.

smelting: A way of removing a metal from its ore by heating the ore until it melts. The molten metal can then be removed and poured into molds, where it cools and solidifies.

supernova: An enormous exploding star, one of the brightest things in the universe.

transition metals: The group of metals that form a block in the middle of the periodic table.

Index